FARMING *in* ULSTER

The Friar's Bush Press gratefully acknowledges the
generous support of the Ulster Folk and Transport
Museum in the original publication of this book.

The Friar's Bush Press
160 Ballylesson Road
Belfast BT8 8JU
Published 1988. Reprinted 2004.
© Copyright reserved
ISBN 0 946872 13 9

Designed by Rodney Miller Associates, Belfast
Printed by W & G Baird, Antrim

FARMING in ULSTER

Historic photographs of Ulster farming and food

Jonathan Bell and Mervyn Watson of
the Ulster Folk and Transport Museum

FRIARS BUSH PRESS

Steam threshing machine, Co. Tyrone, c. 1915 (Cooper collection, D1422/2/6)

During the last 250 years, changes in farming methods have transformed the countryside throughout Europe, and more recently the rest of the world. Ulster farmers have participated in these changes, often very successfully. In common with the rest of Ireland, potatoes and oats were the basic food-crops in Ulster, and cattle, sheep and pigs the most important livestock. However, the relative importance of these crops and livestock has changed over time. Between 1750 and 1850, tillage was of great importance. There were slumps in production, but by the 1820s Ireland had become known as 'the granary of Britain'. After the catastrophic Famine years of the 1840s, however, there was a long-term swing away from tillage, and livestock became much more important. This has remained true in Ulster, even in the specialised farming carried on today.

Within the overall pattern, Ulster farming has had its own distinctive regional character. A clear example of this is the history of pig farming. A pig in the parlour is one of the elements of the music-hall Irish lifestyle, but pork production in Ulster was not only associated with one of the most successful local breeds, the Large White Ulster pig, but it is also a story of economic efficiency. At a domestic level, pigs were fattened both for money and also to enrich the family diet. Commercially pigs were also slaughtered on the home farm before being brought to market. The development of large scale pork production during the last one hundred years shows a relentless drive towards modernisation and competition in international markets, rather than picturesque squalor.

During the last two centuries one crop became strongly associated with Ulster. Flax, and the linen industry, were concentrated in the north of Ireland, and affected not only the rotation of crops, but also the pattern of land-holding. During the late eighteenth century, many Ulster farms were involved in linen production. Small farmers were often also weavers. The amount of labour involved in domestic linen production meant that farmer-weavers could only work very small holdings. The connection between small holdings and linen production aggravated subdivision of farms in the area known as 'linen country'. By the early nineteenth century, this included almost all of Ulster apart from county Fermanagh. The industrialisation of linen manufacture in the nineteenth century removed spinning and weaving from the farms, but holdings remained small, even by Irish standards. Despite consolidation, in 1911 almost 90% of Ulster farms were less than 50 acres, as compared to 84% in Ireland as a whole.

The ways in which farm implements were used in Ulster also had a recognisably local character. During the nineteenth century, a lot of horse-drawn farm equipment was manufactured in huge factories in Britain and America, or in small local foundries such as Kennedy's of Coleraine, or Weir's of Rathfriland. These standardised industrial products, however, were used in distinctive combinations. Most medium-sized Ulster farms had a swing plough, a set of implements for the drill cultivation of potatoes, and sometimes a small reaping-mowing machine. English types of wheel or 'chill' ploughs were often only introduced in the late 1920s – well within living memory.

Ideas for new implements were not all imports. Several Ulster inventions were adopted worldwide. Ferguson's three-point linkage and hydraulic lift system revolutionised tractor design in the 1930s, while J. Hanson's potato digger, patented in 1852, provided a prototype for most later machines. H. Adams' 'Little Wonder' seed fiddle, invented early this century, was not a headline making breakthrough, but nevertheless assisted in what had previously been one of the most tricky tasks on the farm, the even spread of broadcast sown seed.

Ulstermen also made important contributions to the development of other aspects of farming. Sir James Murray carried out pioneering work on the use of superphosphates in Belfast, probably as early as 1808. By 1840 his contribution to their widespread application as fertiliser was internationally recognised. In the present century, Ulster seed potato breeders, such as John Clarke of Broughgammon near Ballycastle, county Antrim, have gained a worldwide reputation for producing new potato varieties.

Many ingenious farming methods used in Ulster were not part of large-scale agriculture, but were developed in response to harsh conditions and limited resources. Poor farmers with tiny holdings, who often did not own a horse, kept their families alive by skills which required simple implements and a lot of manual work. Spadework is the most striking example of this kind of ingenuity. There are hundreds of local types of spade, and even more variation in the techniques of using them. Within any one locality, farmers varied the way they prepared ground in response to changes in the slope of the land, its aspect, the type of soil, crops grown, and their place in the rotation. Even the most ardent champions of large-scale agricultural improvement came to recognise that techniques such as spadework, or reaping grain with a sickle, while slow, hard and labour intensive, also allowed

Lunch break during hay making, c. 1920 (WAG).

thoroughness and neatness which reduced the waste of valuable land and crops. Some efficient techniques required only the bare hands of farm workers. Flax pulling was not successfully mechanised until the 1920s, while lapping hay by hand, a practice particularly associated with the north of Ireland, could save a crop from total destruction in wet weather.

The ingenuity of Ulster farmers in producing food was matched by the skills of farm women in processing it. It is only recently that the variety of dishes produced from simple ingredients has come to be appreciated. Milk was used not only for butter-making, but on some larger farms for making cheese as well. Grain crops were used for baking more types of bread than anywhere else in Ireland, and potatoes were also processed to make food such as potato bread and potato apple cake. The thoroughness with which a pig slaughtered on a farm might be used is remarkable. Not only was bacon cured, and the heart and liver eaten, but the intestines were also often used to make sausages, and in some areas a local variety of haggis was made from the stomach. By the end of the last century, many cottage gardens grew a wide range of vegetables, including garlic, which was widely used, not only as a cure, but also as an ingredient in stews.

During the late nineteenth century, increasingly successful attempts were made to mechanise farming, organise large scale marketing of produce, and to standardise the processing of food. In 1900, an Irish Department of Agriculture and Technical Instruction was set up to achieve these goals. After 1922 this work was carried on in the north by the Northern Ireland Ministry of Agriculture, which had to develop measures, first to cope with the worldwide economic depression, and then to implement national planning to control production both during and after the Second World War. In 1947, an Agriculture Act was passed which became known as 'The Farmers' Charter.' Assured markets and guaranteed prices have been maintained for fat cattle, fat sheep and pigs, liquid milk, wool, eggs, potatoes and cereals. In recent years the Department of Agriculture for Northern Ireland has had the task of integrating Ulster farming into E.E.C. agriculture, and even the smallest farms respond to directives from Brussels.

Rural society has changed as dramatically as farming practices. Until the late nineteenth century, most Ulster farmers were tenants on large estates. Because of tenant right, known as the Ulster Custom, they had more security of tenure than farmers elsewhere in Ireland, but finding money to pay the rent was still a major concern, especially for small farmers. A series of Land Acts, beginning in 1870, meant that by 1925 the system of landholding had almost completely changed, and most Ulster farms were owned by the family working them. Although hiring fairs were still held in some areas right up to the Second World War, hired labour or help from neighbours was only required when there was a shortage of family labour, or where the farm was so big that the family could not cope. On most farms, family labour is still vital.

In recent years, however, a few farming enterprises have become organised on more impersonal commercial lines. The spectacular success of Masstock represents the most successful Ulster venture into 'agribusiness'. Masstock was founded by Alistair and Paddy McGuckian of Massereene Park, county Antrim. In the late 1960s they developed a slatted house system of beef farming, and in the 1970s organised a huge expansion of dairying in Saudi Arabia. Masstock is now a general food resources company with interests in Zambia, China, USA and Thailand. In November 1987 the company further expanded its range of interests with the revolutionary OVAMASS technique of embryo transfer in cattle, developed in conjunction with University College Dublin.

Ironically, as this movement has flourished, a growing awareness of the environmental dangers posed by intensive farming methods, and continued overproduction, has led to attempts to change the emphasis in farming. There is a growing interest in the idea of smaller, diversified, mixed farming, sensitively adjusted to local conditions. If this trend continues, an examination of the success of Ulster farms of this type in the past could provide worthwhile starting points for planning new developments.

Fields & Farms

LANDSCAPE NEAR CUSHENDALL, COUNTY ANTRIM, *c.* 1920 (WAG 135)

For the last two hundred years, most Ulster farms have been small. Until very recently, farming was mixed, a variety of crops and livestock being kept on one farm. The 'patch-work quilt' pattern of most of the landscape was largely a nineteenth century creation. Unenclosed hilly areas were used for common grazing of cattle and sheep.

A FARM AND WINDMILL NEAR MILLISLE, COUNTY DOWN, *c.* 1920 (WAG 1852)

The most prosperous farms in Ulster were in the rich tillage areas, such as the Ards peninsula, and on the rich reclaimed lands to the east of Lough Foyle. The number of outbuildings, and the use of slate for roofs, show that the farm in this photograph was relatively well off.

ISOLATED FARM ON THE SIDE OF SLIEVE BINGNIAN, COUNTY DOWN, *c.* 1920 (WAG 2662)

Around 1750 a rapid increase in population began in Ireland. The cities did not absorb this rise, and country people became increasingly 'land-hungry'. Many poor people moved on to barren bogs and mountains, trying to make a subsistence living for their families. The cultivation of potatoes reached high up in to the hills, but after the potato blight hit the crop in 1845, this method of small-scale land reclamation was largely abandoned. Farmers everywhere began a long-term shift from crops to livestock. Farms which remained viable in the hills, such as the one shown in this photograph, usually depended on sheep.

TURF-WALLED CABIN, COUNTY ANTRIM, *c.* 1920
(WAG 269)

Extreme poverty forced great ingenuity. Thatched cabins walled with turf lasted only a few years. At the end of this time, the collapsed walls were often used for fuel. The cabin in this photography has been propped up to lengthen its life. The window is a mark of relative affluence. The poorest cabins in the nineteenth century had no windows, and no chimneys.

BYRE DWELLING FROM MAGHERAGALLAN,
COUNTY DONEGAL (Modern photo, UFTM, L1236/3)

This photograph is modern, as the house from Gweedore has been re-erected in the grounds of the Ulster Folk and Transport Museum. In byre dwellings, livestock and people lived under the one roof. In 1837 it was claimed that byre dwellings in Gweedore were cleaned out only once a year, when up to 15 tons of animal dung might be removed. This storing up of manure reveals not so much a lack of concern for hygiene, as the vital importance of animal manure for a good potato crop.

DRUMNAHUNSHIN FARM HOUSE (Modern photo, UFTM, L2843/6)

This farm from Armagh, has been re-erected recently in the grounds of the Ulster Folk and Transport Museum. It is typical of many medium sized farm yards during the last hundred years. There are several well-constructed outbuildings, but these are not organised on any rigid plan. The outbuildings – a byre, stables, a poultry house, a dairy, and implement sheds, reflect the mixed farming practice of these farms.

A HAY SHED BEING ERECTED AT SENTRY HILL FARM, CARNMONEY, CO. ANTRIM, 1903 (Dundee Coll, UFTM)

This shed, erected by the Belfast firm Potts and Houston, was entirely metal apart from the wooden truss inside the roof. The shed would have been an indication of prosperity at the turn of the century, but within a few years similar sheds became common features in the Ulster countryside.

Tilling & Sowing

TRANSPORTING MANURE BY SLIPE, *c. 1910 (UM)*

Animal dung was important on all farms, even after the development of artificial fertilisers during the nineteenth century. It was particularly important for farmers depending on potatoes as a subsistence crop. On very small holdings, animal dung was essential if land was to be kept fertile. This photograph shows a Mr Magee of Whiterock, Belfast using a wheelless sledge or slipe.

GATHERING SEAWEED, COUNTY ANTRIM, *c.* 1915
(WAG 1926)

Seaweed was collected and burnt as kelp, and the ash then sold for use in the linen, soap and glass industries. However, all around Ireland, seaweed was also collected for manure. In some areas farmers depended on weed being washed ashore after storms, but elsewhere, for example, along the north shore of Carlingford Lough, lines of stones were deliberately laid out to encourage the growth of seaweed, which was then systematically harvested. The vehicle in this photograph is a solid-wheeled Irish 'car', which survived in use in the Glens of Antrim well within living memory.

MR JOHN DOLAN, OF GLANGEVLIN, CO. CAVAN,
MAKING POTATO RIDGES WITH A ONE-SIDED LOY,
1966 (UFTM L296/13)

*Spadework was the most highly developed manual farming technique
in Ireland. In 1830 one Tyrone spademill produced 230 types of spade.
Spadework was slow, but otherwise very efficient. As recently as the
1940s, most farms of less than 10 acres were cultivated using spades.*

GIRLS COVERING POTATOES, GLENSHESK, CO.
ANTRIM, *c.* 1920s, photograph by R. J. Welch (UM)

On broader ridges, the 'lazy bed' technique of turning sods over onto untilled strips of ground was also used, but the sods formed only the edges of each ridge. The rest of the ridge was built up using loose earth dug from the furrows. On wide ridges such as these, potatoes were often planted three abreast across the ridge. Wider ridges were also used to cultivate oats and flax.

A SWING PLOUGH IN USE IN THE GLENS OF ANTRIM, *c.* 1910 (UM)

Horse ploughs changed greatly during the eighteenth and nineteenth centuries. By 1800, improvers were successfully persuading Irish farmers to use Scottish swing ploughs. These ploughs remained very popular in Ulster until the 1930s. The ploughman had to control not only the horses, but also the depth and width of the furrow being turned by the plough. This required great skill, but meant that on hilly or stony ground, the ploughman could avoid obstacles, or lessen the strain on the horses on steep slopes. Swing ploughs are still sometimes used in the Glens of Antrim, but sadly the sturdy Cushendall hill ponies shown in this photograph are now extinct.

A SWING PLOUGH IN USE ON A LARGE LOWLAND
FARM, *c.* 1915 (WAG 291)

*Swing ploughs were so popular that they were made in large numbers
in local foundries. Gray's of Belfast was the largest manufacturer, but
local blacksmiths also made ploughs, using basic components made in
the foundries.*

BLACKSMITH'S FORGE WITH SWING PLOUGH
WAITING FOR ADJUSTMENT, *c.* 1910 (UM)

Rural blacksmiths made and repaired most farmers' tools. However, only the most skilled blacksmiths were able to make and set a swing plough. Even though the blacksmith assembled the swing plough he was not able to make all the parts. The share and mould board had to be cast in a foundry. Later horse drawn, foundry made ploughs, with standardised, detachable parts, did not require the services of the local blacksmith.

A WHEEL PLOUGH IN USE, *c.* 1920 (WAG 1981)

Standardised mass produced wheel ploughs with detachable parts were first developed in England by the English firm, Ransome's of Ipswich, in 1808. This type of plough was most quickly adopted on larger, lowland farms in Ulster. The wheels at the front of the plough could be used to control the depth and width of the furrow being turned. Detachable parts meant that farmers no longer needed to consult the local blacksmith if they broke the plough, as replacement parts were readily available and could be fitted by the farmer himself.

Standardisation also meant that ploughs manufactured in different foundries often had interchangeable parts. For example in 1950, some ploughs manufactured in the Wexford Engineering Works could be fitted with parts made by the British firms, Ransome, Howard, Hornsby and Sellar, and the American firm, Oliver.

PLOUGHING WITH A 'FORDSON' MOTOR TRACTOR,
c. 1917 (WAG 1982)

Some Ulster farmers began to use tractors during the First World
War, when the government's 'compulsory tillage' policy made the
investment worthwhile. Early tractors, however, were of limited use
because implements were simply dragged behind the machine, which
meant that the driver had very little control over their operation.

FERGUSON TRACTORS PLOUGHING, *c.* 1940 (UFTM, L2848/1)

Ulster's most famous agricultural inventor began to develop his revolutionary tractor design during the First World War. Ferguson's major contribution was the three point linkage and hydraulic lift at the back of the tractor, which meant that the driver could also control the movement of an implement attached to the machine. Ferguson's designs were not commercially produced until 1936, when the Ferguson Brown 'Type A' tractors were manufactured by David Brown of Huddersfield.

HARROWING AND SOWING SEED, *c.* 1920 (WAG 262)

The sharp teeth or 'tines' of harrows are used to break up ground after ploughing, or to mix soil and newly-sown seed together. Most improved harrows were made in two frames or 'leaves', which allowed the implement to rise and fall with the irregularities in the ground.

On many Ulster farms, where only a small acreage of cereals was grown, sowing seed by hand, or 'broadcasting' was common well into the present century.

A SEED FIDDLE BEING USED TO SOW GRAIN, *c.* 1920
(WAG 3101A)

Seed was poured into the bag and the attached box held under the sower's arm. The 'bow' of the fiddle made a metal disc below the box rotate. As seed fell onto the disc, it was flung in a wide arc around the sower. If he walked at a regular pace, and pushed and pulled the bow at an even rate, all of the ground would be covered.

27

Potatoes

A MOURNE PLOUGH IN USE, *c.* 1920 (UFTM, L2831/4)

Cultivating crops in long straight rows, or drills, means that horse drawn implements can be used more effectively for planting, weeding, and harvest. Since the late eighteenth century, drills have been commonly used in Ireland for growing potatoes. In the Mourne mountains, farmers adapted their old wooden ploughs so that they could build up drills. This led to the development of a distinctive series of wooden 'Mourne' ploughs. This photograph shows Samuel Forsythe, of Ballinnan near Kilkeel, operating a plough made by Archie Orr of Kilkeel. William and Sam Forsythe are planting the seed.

SETTING POTATOES IN DRILLS, *c.* 1910 (UM)
*The boy in this photograph is wearing a 'guggerin'' bag in which
potato seed was carried. Planting potatoes was a job frequently given
to young people of both sexes.*

EXPERIMENTAL POTATO SPRAYING, 1930s (UFTM 11483/7)

Potato blight (Phytophthora infestans) hit Ireland in 1845, 1846, and 1847. It was a fungus which made potatoes vulnerable to other diseases, causing rotting. Over a million people died in the Famine brought on by the blight, and attacks of blight in later years continued to increase hardship and emigration. The first sprays preventing blight were developed in France in the 1880s. Spraying was well established in Ulster by 1900, but blight attacks remain an ongoing problem.

POTATO DIGGER, 1985 (UFTM L1482/9)

Mechanical potato diggers were fitted with a large blade which cut beneath the tubers growing in drills. Revolving forks at the back of the machine then kicked the tubers out of the ground so that harvest workers following behind simply had to collect them. The prototype of this kind of machine was patented by J. Hanson of Doagh, Co Antrim in 1852. Mr Bertie Hanna of Saintfield is harvesting the potato crop at the Ulster Folk and Transport Museum in the photograph here.

STORING POTATOES NEAR NEWCASTLE, COUNTY
DOWN, *c.* 1915 (WAG 280)
*Potatoes stored in bings or pits could be kept fresh all winter. The
heap of potatoes was covered with straw, and then a covering of earth.
The end of the bing could be opened and potatoes removed as required.
The men in this photograph are James Kendall, and his son William.*

IRISH WOMEN HARVESTING POTATOES IN
AYRSHIRE, SCOTLAND, AROUND 1900 (UFTM
L2331/7)

Many Ulster farm servants came from the west of county Donegal. Young Donegal people often worked on farms further east in Ulster as a first stage in a career of migrant labour. After several years they went on to work in the Scottish potato harvest as 'tattie hokers', before coming back to the family farm in Donegal, or emigrating permanently.

Flax

FLAX PULLING NEAR CUSHENDUN, COUNTY
ANTRIM, *c.* 1915 (WAG 1011)

*By early this century most Ulster linen was manufactured from
imported flax. However, especially during the World Wars, some local
cultivation continued. The fibres in flax stalks are so strong that
scythes or reaping machines cannot cut through them. Pulling was an
efficient harvesting technique because it also meant that the entire
length of the fibres in the flax stalks was saved. Once pulled, the flax
was bound in sheaves or 'beets' using bands of rushes.*

RIPPLING FLAX, COUNTY ANTRIM, *c.* 1915
(WAG 1024)

Bolls containing seed could be removed from the flax by pulling the stalks through a large iron comb. Experts disagreed as to whether leaving the seed on the flax lessened the quality of the fibre during processing. Since most Ulster farmers grew flax for its fibre rather than for seed, many left the bolls on the stalks, rather than undertake the labour of rippling.

REMOVING RETTED FLAX FROM THE LINT-HOLE
NEAR CUSHENDUN, COUNTY ANTRIM, *c*. 1915
(WAG 1062)

Flax dams were made long and narrow, and the 'beets' of flax were often piled in two layers under the stagnant water. The length of time flax was left in the water depended on temperature. The object of steeping flax, to rot the central woody part or 'shous' of the stalk, might take between one and two weeks. The stench of retted flax was notorious and the water was poisonous to fish, but some farmers claim that cattle loved flax water, which made them drunk! This photograph was taken on the McSparran's farm in Cloney townland. The men in the photograph are (from left to right), Mr John Hamilton a cousin of Mr McSparran, John McKillop and John O'Neill, two local men hired on the farm as day-labourers, and Daniel McLoughlin, a 'foreman' on the McSparran's farm, who died in 1919.

SPREADING RETTED FLAX TO DRY, *c.* 1915
(WAG 1015)

After flax was taken out of a dam or 'lint-hole', the 'beets' were set upright for a few hours to drain, and the flax was then spread to dry. Drying might take anything between 6 days and a fortnight. A farmer could tell that the flax was dry when the stalks began to form a 'string and bow' caused by the fibres contracting from the woody central stalk.

37

LINT WHEEL FOR BRUISING FLAX, COUNTY
DONEGAL, *c.* 1915 (WAG 1069)

*Processing flax for linen was complicated and labour-intensive. After
retting and drying, the woody stalks and fibres were separated by
scutching. This was often preceded by the method of 'bruising' flax*
*shown here. The large stone wheel broke up the woody stalks so that
they were more easily beaten out from the fibres during scutching.*

FLAX PULLING MACHINE, 1940s (UFTM, L1585/11)

The first successful machines for pulling flax were developed in the 1920s. During the 1940s, the Belfast firm, James Mackie and Sons Ltd., manufactured machines which pulled flax, as in this photograph, by means of two continuous belts running together. However, the use of these machines coincided with the virtual disappearance of flax as a crop in Ulster.

Hay & Grain

**HAYMAKERS NEAR THE BRACKENRIDGE
MONUMENT, COUNTY TYRONE, *c.* 1910 (RS)**

*At busy times of the year, farmers sometimes hired temporary 'day
labourers', or called on neighbours for help. Groups of helpers were
sometimes called a* meitheal, *a 'gathering,' or a 'fiddler.' The last
term was used because after the work was finished, the farmer who
had been helped would often arrange a dance as a celebration.*

A FIELD OF HAY LAPS IN WESTERN IRELAND,
AROUND 1900 (UFTM, L2220/6)

Improvers criticised Irish farmers for leaving cut hay too long in the field. They pointed out that the longer hay lay out, the more likely nutrients were to be washed away, and also that the hay would eventually rot. Farmers responded that the damper Irish climate and lusher grass meant that mown grass took longer to dry than in England. Lapping, or making hay into small rolls, was an ingenious practice particularly associated with the northern half of Ireland, which protected hay in damp conditions. Water tended to run off the rolls, while air circulating through them assisted drying.

A RUCK-SHIFTER IN A FARMYARD NEAR
BALLYWALTER, COUNTY DOWN (UFTM L2726/10)

*By 1900, hay was the most widely cultivated crop in Ireland. The
photograph, taken during the 1930s, shows Mr William Lyons on his
farm at Ganaway. Ruck shifters had large, flat bodies and a winching
mechanism fitted on front, which meant that a whole heap of hay
could be moved on to the cart at once.*

PADDY STOREY REAPING OATS WITH A SICKLE,
NEAR TOOME, COUNTY ANTRIM, *c.* 1920 (WAG 298)

For hundreds of years, the toothed sickle (corrán cíorach) was the standard Irish tool for harvesting grain. Holding each handful of grain as it was being cut meant that seed was not shaken out of the heads, and also meant that some weeds growing among the crop could be left behind. The technique was very efficient and in the nineteenth century many English farmers preferred to hire large squads of Irish reapers, than local, more expensive, scythesmen.

REAPING AND BINDING OATS, COUNTY TYRONE, *c.*
1910 (RS 360)
Sickles and hooks were used by both men and women. Hooks could be used in the same way as sickles, but also for slashing, a less neat but quicker way of harvesting. As with scythes, however, hooks require frequent sharpening while in use. The women in this picture are Mary and Ellen McCaughey, of Corleaghan.

HARVESTING OATS IN COUNTY TYRONE, *c.* 1910
(UFTM L918/8)

The man in the background of this photograph is sharpening a scythe with a board known as a strickle. Mowing grain only became common in Ireland during the late nineteenth century, although some hay had been mown on large estates since Norman times.

The two girls shown here are binding four sheaves of oats into a stook which was sometimes called a 'pirlin''. These small stooks were often made in damp conditions, because they allowed air to circulate easily around the grain and straw in the sheaves.

HARVESTING OATS WITH A REAPING MACHINE
NEAR TOOME, COUNTY ANTRIM, *c.* 1920 (WAG 1158)

An experimental reaping machine was demonstrated at Moira, County Down, in 1806, but it was not until 1852 when American Hussey and McCormick reapers where displayed at the Royal Ulster Agricultural Show, that wealthier farmers began to invest in the machines. As with scythes, the increased speed at which reaping machines operated meant that more workers were required to bind the sheaves. In this photograph women are binding the sheaves, and a man is making stooks.

THE CEREMONIAL CUTTING OF A LAST SHEAF, NEAR TOOME, COUNTY ANTRIM, *c.* 1920 (WAG 1160)

The last sheaf of standing grain was called by many names, including cailleach *('old woman'), 'chirn', 'hare', or 'hag'. In most areas it was thought lucky to be the reaper who cut the sheaf, but it was sometimes claimed that the reaper would be dead within a year. The last sheaf ceremony marked the start of harvest celebrations in farmhouses and in church.*

A 'HARVEST HOME' MEAL, TOOME, COUNTY
ANTRIM, *c. 1920* (WAG 1162)

*Celebration meals, sometimes known as a 'chirn', were arranged on
many farms at the end of the grain harvest. The family, farm workers,
and neighbours would often be included. In this photograph the plaited
'last sheaf' of oats has been hung over the table.*

THRESHING OATS WITH FLAILS, NEAR TOOME COUNTRY ANTRIM, *c.* 1920 (WAG 296)

The flails being used in this photograph are the most common type found in Ulster. The tying joining the 'striker' or 'souple' to the handstaff, passes through a hole in the latter. This meant that the beater could not swing freely around unless the handstaff was turned in the worker's hands. By 1900, flailing was usually done indoors, during long winter evenings.

A BARN THRESHING MACHINE IN USE, *c.* 1920
(WAG 1959)

Machines for threshing grain were developed in Scotland during the
late eighteenth century. Revolving beaters knocked seed out of grain,
before the straw was carried out by revolving spikes in the larger drum
at the rear of the machine.

A HORSE WALK FOR OPERATING A BARN
THRESHING MACHINE, *c.* 1910 (UM)

Horses were harnessed to a gearing mechanism, which was turned as they walked around it. The gears were connected to the threshing machine inside the barn by an underground driving shaft. Agricultural writers condemned early horse powered machines as cruel, claiming that a machine driven by four horses required the effort of three of them simply to turn the gears. Later, lighter machines made the work less heavy.

A STEAM THRESHING MACHINE IN USE (UM)

Steam threshing machines were first exhibited in Ireland during the 1850s. Very few farmers could afford to buy a machine, so most would hire one, along with the engine driver, for several days afer harvest.

At least ten men were required to operate the larger machines. This labour problem was solved by neighbours joining together to work on each of their farms in turn, until all of their grain was threshed.

WINNOWING GRAIN IN THE OPEN AIR, *c.* 1915 (WAG 277)

Machines for winnowing, or removing the husks from grain, were developed in Holland and Scotland during the eighteenth century. Well into the present century, however, some Ulster farmers winnowed in the open air, using a breeze to blow the light shells away. The seed was poured from a tray made from animal skin stretched around a wooden frame. In the north of Ireland these trays were known as wechts, wights or dalláin, *but in the south as* bodhráin.

GRINDING OATS WITH A SADDLE QUERN, COUNTY
ANTRIM, *c.* 1920 (WAG 1962)

Querns of several types have a very long history in Ireland. By the mid-nineteenth century, most areas had a corn mill, often built by the local landlord, where grain could be ground on a large scale. Small *hand querns survived in use, however, when small amounts of flour were required, or when oats were being crushed to feed to livestock such as poultry.*

OAT CAKES MADE OVER A TURF FIRE, *c.* 1920
(WAG 1163)

In many Irish houses cooking was done over an open fire until well into the present century. In this photograph an oatcake is baking on a griddle and three others are propped around the fire for hardening. The griddle is suspended from a crane which could be adjusted vertically or horizontally. Women judged the correct height to hang the griddle by the colour of the burning turf, or by passing their hands between the griddle and the flame.

Livestock

POUNDING GORSE FOR ANIMAL FODDER, 1960s
(UFTM, L521/7)

Fodder used to supplement livestock's diet of hay or grass included not only potatoes and other root crops, but also hedgerow plants such as holly, ivy, or as in this photograph, gorse. The branches of gorse were placed on a large flat stone and smashed with wooden mallets known as mells. Gorse was thought to make horses' coats shine with health.

However, one popular belief urged that all horses on a farm should be fed gorse at the same time. If a horse which had eaten gorse was harnessed to one which had not, the latter would become sick or even die if its partner breathed on it!

IRISH DRAUGHT STALLION, 1903 (UFTM, L2853/6)

Some Ulster farmers used small cobs or ponies for farm work, and on some large farms Clydesdale horses were popular. However, many farmers preferred a medium sized horse such as the Irish Draught, which could be used for draught or riding. Horses of this general type were often known as 'clean-bones', because their feet were smaller than Clydesdales, and their lower legs not so hairy. This made it easier for them to walk neatly in a furrow, or between drills, and also meant that their lower legs were easier to clean.

SHEEP DIPPING, COUNTY ANTRIM, *c.* 1920
(WAG 1945)

The home production of wool is a very ancient practice in Ireland.
Sheep farming became very important in hilly districts during the later
nineteenth century, especially when subsistence farms left, or were
removed, from marginal land. The chemical solution in which sheep
are dipped, kills parasites living in their fleece.

SHEEP IN THE MOURNE MOUNTAINS, *c.* 1920
(WAG 1723)

*These blackface mountain sheep, which can still be found in the
Mournes, have longer legs and slightly finer coats than the more
common, Scottish blackface breed. Mourne sheep are good for mutton,
and in the early years of the present century, this was exported to
restaurants as far away as Paris.*

FEEDING CHICKENS NEAR THE MOY, COUNTY TYRONE, 1899 (UM)

Poultry flocks on most farms were in the care of the women. Women fed the birds, but also kept the money made from the sale of eggs. This could be a significant amount, since even on small farms up to a hundred birds might be kept, and it was estimated that forty chickens were equal in value to a cow.

UNLADING A CART LOAD OF EGGS (700 DOZ) IN COOKSTOWN MARKET. WAG 1901.

UNLOADING EGGS AT COOKSTOWN MARKET,
COUNTY TYRONE, *c.* 1920 (WAG 1901)
*Organisations like co-operative societies and the Department of
Agriculture aimed to standardise and upgrade farm produce. Some
Irish women opposed efforts to organise the egg trade, because they
saw it as an attempt by men to take away one of their major sources of
money.*

'HIVING' A SWARM OF BEES IN A STRAW 'SKEP', *c.* 1920 (WAG 1980)

Bee-keeping has a very long history in Ireland, but at the beginning of the century, some government backed organisations tried to increase the production of honey as part of mixed farming. The Irish Beekeepers' Association was formed in 1881, and is still going strong.

LARGE WHITE ULSTER PIG, AT CASTLEWELLAN MARKET, COUNTY DOWN, *c.* 1915 (WAG 1175)

Pigs became an important part of the Irish small farming economy during the last two centuries. In some areas, the pig was known as 'the gentleman who pays the rent', as selling a fattened pig was an important source of cash income. The Large White Ulster pig is thought to have been developed by local farmers during the nineteenth century for the roll bacon and ham trade, which had extensive export markets in the north of England and the industrial areas of Scotland. Unfortunately, the Large White Ulster was a fat type of pig with a high ratio of fat to lean. A growing preference for leaner bacon, and centralization of pork production led to its decline as the main pig used by Ulster farmers in pig production, and its eventual extinction.

SHAVING THE HAIR OFF A NEWLY SLAUGHTERED
PIG, 1895 (Dundee Coll. UFTM)

*Pig production in Ulster was mainly based on a dead pork trade.
Until the middle years of the present century, in Ulster, pig
slaughtering generally took place on the farm. The most common
method involved stunning the pig and cutting its throat. Once the pig
had been slaughtered and bled, the carcase was usually placed in a tub
of boiling water or 'scald' to make the coat or hair easier to remove.
The carcase was then lifted out of the scald and placed on a suitable
board where the pig killer shaved the hair off. Here, pig killer, Tom
Couley is shaving the hair off a Large White Ulster pig on the
McKinney farm, Co Antrim, c. 1900. After the hair had been
removed the carcase was hung up, split and the innards removed.
Parts of the innards or pluck were kept by Ulster farmers for domestic
use. These were usually the heart and liver, which were eaten, and
sometimes the stomach, which was stuffed to make a local form of
haggis, and the intestines, which were used for sausage casings.*

PIG MARKET, ARMAGH, 1900 (UM)

In this photograph cart loads of pig carcases are lined up at the weighing scales in Armagh pig market. Prior to the setting up of the Pig Marketing Scheme in 1933, and the subsequent spread of curing establishments with killing facilities, pigs slaughtered on the farm were taken to market by horse and cart. At the market local agents or buyers from the various bacon curing firms purchased the carcases from the farmers. This system of marketing was open to abuses, usually at the expense of the farmer, and was characterised by dramatic fluctuations in prices. The Pig Marketing Scheme was set up in 1933 with a view to simplify marketing and stabilise prices.

Dairying & Markets

SHORTHORN CATTLE, *c.* 1915 (WAG 1713)

Some attempts were made during the late nineteenth century to develop 'dual-purpose' cattle breeds in Ireland. These could be used either for milk or beef. The best known of the local breeds of this kind were Irish moils (hornless cattle) and Kerry cattle. However, shorthorn cows were the type most widely kept on small or medium farms. On very small holdings, owning a cow was not only important for milk and beef, but also for manure.

MILKING A SHORTHORN COW, COUNTY ANTRIM,
c. 1915 (WAG 1952)

The woman in this picture, Mrs McCollum, from near Cushendun,
would most likely have milked her cow indoors. This outdoor
arrangement was probably to make it easier to photograph the task.
Cows were milked twice a day, morning and evening.

MILKING AT GREENMOUNT AGRICULTURAL
COLLEGE, COUNTY ANTRIM, *c.* 1920s (WAG 3204)

*Greenmount College was established in 1912 with an intake of eleven
students. In 1988 there were 230, both men and women. Even before
mechanisation was widespread, the large-scale organisation of milking
cattle meant that yields could be measured with a view to
improvement, and the quality of milk tested.*

CHURNING BUTTER, COUNTY ANTRIM, *c.* 1915
(WAG 295)

Buttermaking on the farm was usually women's work. Milk was stored in pans or crocks until soured. In the north of Ireland, many women churned the 'whole milk' rather than just cream. This was harder work, but provided a good supply of buttermilk for baking. On small farms, most butter made was eaten by the family. Before the development of creameries extra butter could be sold to local shops, or 'butter merchants,' who travelled from farm to farm.

COUNTY TYRONE CREAMERY, *c.* 1910 (Cooper, D1422/9/5)

By 1915 there were 143 co-operative creameries in Ulster. The Irish Agricultural Organisation Society, which was the central body of the Irish co-operative movement hoped that every farmer who had a cow would join a creamery. In the creamery the milk was tested for quality and then put through a 'separator' which produced cream, and skim milk. In the early days of co-ops the society bought the cream, while the skimmed milk and some buttermilk was given back to the farmer. Skimmed milk was generally used for fattening pigs for market.

A BELFAST CO-OPERATIVE SOCIETY VAN, 1913
(UFTM, L1753/11)

*Belfast Co-op was founded in May 1889 with 199 members. By 1919,
the membership was over 21,300 and the society had a turnover of
over one million pounds. It is a retail co-op, organised chiefly to sell
goods at cheap prices to industrial workers.*

MILK AND BREAD SOLD BY BELFAST CO-OP IN 1913
(UFTM, L1754/15)
Standardisation and large-scale marketing allowed hygienic practices,
and also the availability of fresh food to large numbers of city people.

SELLING MILK IN BELFAST, 1913 (UFTM, L1754/3)

The Belfast Co-op had its own dairy farm near Belfast, but it was also the largest buyer of Northern Ireland creamery butter. During the 1920s, the society's support helped to reverse the decline in dairy farming in Ulster. This is a rare, but unfortunately damaged photograph.

PORTADOWN FRUIT AND VEGETABLE BOTTLING
AND DRYING EXHIBIT IN DUBLIN, 1904 (UFTM,
L2848/4)

*By the beginning of the present century Ulster's provision trade had
developed a high standard of packaging and presentation suitable for
large-scale marketing.*

W. R. RANGECROFT'S SHOP AT 229 ANTRIM ROAD,
APRIL 1931, by Alex Hogg (UM, H10/35/8)
The country feeds the city. A lot of the provisions on sale in this shop
would have been produced on Ulster farms. By this date, however,
food was also being imported, from all over the world.

INSPECTING POTATOES BEFORE THEY WERE
EXPORTED, BELFAST DOCKS, 1939 by Alex Hogg (UM)
The Northern Ireland Ministry of Agriculture introduced several
marketing schemes in the 1930s, which ensured minimum standards of
quality. Farm produce improved, and potatoes became a major
agricultural export, both as food and for seed.

FAIR DAY IN ANTRIM, 1924 (WAG 2122)

Despite large-scale developments in the food trade, weekly markets and monthly fairs remained the most important way in which country people sold produce and bought supplies, until well into the present century. Bartering goods persisted in some small markets until within living memory.

HIRING FAIR AT BALLYMONEY, COUNTY ANTRIM, *c.* 1910 (UFTM)

Early this century many small Ulster towns had hiring fairs around the 12th May and 12th November. Hired servants usually lived on the farm where they worked, for a 'term' of six months. They often carried a 'bundle' containing their belongings to the fair and gave this to the farmer who employed them, in return for a small payment known as an 'earls' or 'earnest', which sealed the contract. Wages were not paid until the end of the term, but most servants judged their employers by living conditions on the farm, especially food. Hired people remembered conditions varying from 'slavery' to being 'treated as one of the family.'*

SOME STATISTICS RELATED TO ULSTER FARMING

1. *Size of farms*

Between 1841 and 1851 the number of holdings of one to five acres declined by two thirds.

Between 1851 and 1914 farms of over 30 acres gradually increased in numbers.

However, even in the first half of this century:

38% of all farms were less than 15 acres.
83% of all farms were less than 50 acres.

Only 4% of farms were larger than 100 acres. In England and Wales 21% of farms were larger than 100 acres.

2. *The decline of tillage in Ulster, 1850–1900*

	Wheat	Oats	Barley	Potatoes	Turnips	Flax	Meadow
1850	53,084	854,794	51,745	299,629	114,188	160,300	282,169
1900	17,535	535,255	6,819	264,756	102,731	46,929	592,923

3. *The increase in livestock in Ulster, 1850–1900*

	Horses	Cattle	Sheep	Pigs	Goats	Poultry
1850	149,818	1,023,961	316,920	296,513	57,461	2,783,609
1900	180,267	1,203,449	644,555	341,498	80,326	6,896,032

By the 1930s 80% of the value of agricultural output in Northern Ireland came from livestock and livestock products.

Sources

THOM's *Directory of Ireland* 1853, 1901 (Dublin).
Ministry of Agriculture (N.I.) *Monthly Reports* 1931 (Belfast).

Acknowledgements

Eleven photographs in this book are reproduced by kind permission of the Ulster Museum. Mr Robert Heslip of the Local History Department was especially helpful in drawing our attention to the large collection of photographs relating to agriculture in the museum's archives. Two photographs are reproduced from the Dundee collection, while the photograph of the ruck-shifter near Ballywalter was donated to the Ulster Folk and Transport archives by Dolly McRoberts and Isobel Lyons. Two photographs are reproduced by kind permission of the Deputy Keeper of the Records, Public Record Office of Northern Ireland.

Thanks, as usual, go to the Ulster Folk and Transport Museum's photographers, Ken Anderson, Alan McCartney and George Wright, who always produce the goods.

The photographers

Most photographs reproduced from the Ulster Folk and Transport Museum's archives were taken by W. A. Green (WAG) and two by Rose Shaw (RS): the Dundee collection, the work of W. F. McKinney, provided two photographs. Those from the archives of the Ulster Museum (UM) include the work of F. J. Biggar, Alex Hogg and R. J. Welch. The two photographs from the Cooper collection (P.R.O.N.I.) are the work of J. W. Burrows.

Further reading

BELL, Jonathan and WATSON, Mervyn *Irish farming* (Edinburgh, 1986).
EVANS, Estyn *Irish Folkways* (London, 1957, 1967, 1988).
IRWIN, Florence *The Cookin' Woman* (London, 1949, Belfast, 1986).
Ulster Folklife vols 1–34 (Belfast, 1955–1988).